Life-Changing Classics, Volume XXXVII

COMMON HORSE SENSE
FROM WILL ROGERS

SEVEN TIMELESS TIPS FOR LEADERS

(AND EVERYONE ELSE)

I0894207

Jennifer Rogers & Randall Reeder

TREMENDOUS LEADERSHIP
Leadership with a kick!

Tremendous Leadership
PO Box 267 • Boiling Springs, PA 17007
(717) 701 - 8159 • (800) 233 - 2665
www.TremendousLeadership.com

Tremendous Leadership's titles may be purchased in bulk for business, promotional, or special sales. Please contact Tremendous Leadership for more information.

Cover photo courtesy of the Will Rogers Memorial Museum. Used with permission.

Paperback ISBN: 978-1-961202-49-8
eBook ISBN: 978-1-961202-47-4

DESIGNED & PRINTED IN THE
UNITED STATES OF AMERICA

TABLE OF CONTENTS

INTRODUCTION

Was Will Rogers a leader? Not in the way we usually identify leaders. He was never CEO of a big company or even a tiny one, never president of an organization, and never had more than four employees—unless you include horses or his short time as the honorary

Mayor of Beverly Hills. Will Rogers was an entertainer who also wrote syndicated newspaper columns.

You've probably heard, "You don't have to have a title to be a leader." So, even if you don't see yourself as a leader, these examples from Will Rogers' life show positive examples that may inspire you to also become a leader.

"Servant leaders," like Will Rogers, have empathy for others. Many of those "served" are close by: co-workers, friends, and family. Others may be unknown personally, locally, across the country, or around the world.

With or without a title, leaders can help others develop and grow their own talents. They can also create opportunities for growth, especially among young people, and inspire them to broaden their horizons. Will said, "America is the land of opportunity, and don't ever forget it." Leaders help others set higher goals and reach them.

So, who was this "Will Rogers?" William Penn Adair Rogers was born on November 4,

1879, and grew up on a ranch at Oologah in Indian Territory, now the state of Oklahoma. He was a quarter-blood Cherokee and proud of it. He attended six different schools, the last one being Kemper Military Academy in Boonville, Missouri. He left school for good with the equivalent of a tenth-grade education, but he never stopped learning.

Will became a world-class trick roper, and that amazing skill got him on Vaudeville stages. He took advantage of opportunities, which got him invited to star in movies, write syndicated newspaper columns, and have a network radio show.

Will Rogers was an entertainer and common horse sense thinker. A key to his success was Betty Blake. After an eight-year on-and-off romance, they got married in 1908. Both were 29 years old.

Will knew many prominent leaders personally. He learned a lot about leadership and shared those tips with his "audiences" through newspaper columns, radio broadcasts, and presentations in theaters across the country.

Will said, "Henry Ford has always had more common sense than anybody." He complimented President Calvin Coolidge, "You put horse sense into statesmanship." He also praised President Herbert Hoover, who was an engineer: "I always did want to see him elected. I wanted to see how far a competent man could go in politics. It has never been tried before."

He opposed racism and did not appreciate politicians who supported segregation. He promoted the idea of an old-age pension (which became Social Security in 1935) and "relief for the farmer." The first Farm Bill was signed in 1933. Will was an early supporter of aviation. Ironically, he died, along with famed pilot Wiley Post, when their plane lost power and crashed at Point Barrow, Alaska, on August 15, 1935.

From his start, entertaining at "Wild West Shows," Will moved to Vaudeville, and ultimately became a star on the "Cadillac" of vaudeville shows, the Ziegfeld Follies, in 1916. Starting in 1918, Will appeared in 50 silent movies.

In 1929, he made the first of 21 "talkies" (movies with sound). The producers and directors, including Oscar-winning John Ford, gave Will complete freedom to change scripts and alter scenes. Will used that freedom to promote the growth of fellow actors, including Lincoln Perry, known as Stepin' Fetchit, Bill Robinson, known as Bojangles, and Henry B. Walthall. Will Rogers created situations where these three actors could grow beyond what was expected of them.

Without a title, Will Rogers lived his life as a role model for leaders (and everyone else). "Live your life so that whenever you lose, you are ahead." When Will wrote that in 1931, he added, "Get a few laughs, do the best you can."

Once, on the "lecture circuit," Will left his hotel to walk to the theater in time to go on stage. Outside the theater, a group of black kids, teenagers, and probably a few adults were standing on the sidewalk, hoping to get a chance to see the famous Will Rogers. You might guess that a star performer will greet the group briefly and move on. But not Will. He pulled out his lassos and gave them a free show for at least 30 minutes while the folks inside impatiently waited for him to take the stage. Why did Will do this? The theater was segregated. Those young Blacks were not allowed to go inside.

Will had no desire to amass wealth. He was generous with friends and strangers alike. For example, in 1928, he substituted several weeks for his good friend, Fred Stone, in a Broadway play after Fred broke both legs in an accident. After each show, when Will left by the stage door, several unemployed actors and beggars usually waited. He always prepared a roll of dollar bills that he distributed.

By 1933, he was the top male box-office attraction and highest-paid actor. As he left each morning to work on a movie, Betty would give him money, knowing he would give a few dollars to anyone who looked like they needed it. When he returned for supper, his pockets would be empty. Will did invest in property. He said (paraphrased), "Buy land because they aren't making any more of it." He advised a young, handsome actor, Joel McCrea, to buy land (details in Chapter 1.)

Will and Betty purchased a three-quarter mile stretch of Pacific Ocean beach at Santa Monica, and over 300 acres of hillside property at Pacific Palisades. Instead of making millions from selling those valuable properties, the family gave them to the state of California. The beach is now called Will Rogers State Beach. Additionally, 186 acres of that hillside, purchased in the mid-1920s, is now known as Will Rogers State Historic Park. Unfortunately, on January 7, 2025, a major fire destroyed the house (and classic horse barn) and burned approximately 60,000 acres of Pacific Palisades and other

L.A. suburbs. Months later, the future of Will Rogers State Historic Park is still in question. Will's reputation clearly lives on as his great-granddaughter, Jennifer Rogers, received many supportive phone calls and emails from all around the world.

CHAPTER 1

THOUGHT LEADER AND INFLUENCER

The term "thought leader" did not exist a hundred years ago, but Will Rogers was one. For example, while on the "speaking circuit," Will wanted to do radio interviews to promote the shows. Theater owners objected, thinking that if people could hear Will talk for free on a radio interview, they wouldn't want to pay for a ticket to see him in person.

Of course, the opposite was true. Ticket sales increased when radio listeners heard Will's jovial manner and fresh humor. Will was a multi-media star. He wrote a weekly syndicated newspaper article (starting in 1922) and a daily newspaper item, "Will Rogers Says," or Daily Telegrams (starting in 1927). He was a movie star. There's no better way to sell tickets to an upcoming live performance than to be famous and "in front of" people frequently.

Note: In this book, quotes from his newspaper columns are referenced. Weekly Articles are abbreviated WA, and Daily Telegrams are DT.

On his network radio programs (Sunday night, 15 minutes), Will was unscripted. He usually wrote notes, and sometimes discussed the topic he planned to cover with his wife, Betty. Other programs at that time were fully scripted, such as "Amos and Andy." After doing a couple of radio shows without a live audience, Will had the network invite one. A humorous speaker knows how valuable it is to have laughter and other reactions. Well-known people attended in the audience, and often Will would interview them, the beginning of "talk radio."

Will Rogers was an Influencer. He did not have Twitter (X), TikTok, or Instagram to build a massive list of followers he could "influence." But Will wrote and spoke common sense in the language of the people. Leaders in business and government paid attention to Will's wisdom.

Humorous speakers and comedians continue to credit Will for techniques that are guaranteed to generate more laughs. One example is adding one, two, or even three laugh lines after the main punch line. Will also prepared and memorized "saver lines," for when a joke does not get a laugh.

In one case, Will typed ten saver lines he could use "extemporaneously" if a rope trick did not work. Sometimes, he would intentionally mess up a rope trick because he knew the "ad-lib" line would get a big laugh. Will was skilled at ad-libbing, even if it wasn't pre-planned.

A newspaper columnist, Henry L. Mencken, complained about Will's influence on our leaders. He denounced Will Rogers to his face as "the most influential editorial writer in America. He alters foreign policies. He makes and unmakes candidates. He destroys public figures. By deriding Congress and undermining its prestige he has virtually reduced us to a monarchy. Millions of American free men read his words daily, and those who are unable to read listen to him over the radio.... I consider him the most dangerous writer alive today." (St. Louis Post-Dispatch, June 11, 1928)

Will responded, "Come on, now, Henry, you know that nobody with any sense ever took any of my gags seriously."

Mencken replied, "Certainly not. They are taken seriously by nobody except half-wits, in other words by approximately 85 percent of the voting population."

Despite Mencken's shouting, this exchange may have been partly 'for show.' He and Will were friends and continued the give-and-take of men who understand each other.

Will influenced President Franklin D. Roosevelt and Congress. Will wanted the government to provide a $200-a-month pension for old folks. "With all the haywire ideas we have, every once in a while, we hit on a good one like old age pensions, which is sure to come at the next Congress" (DT #2585, November 18, 1934). The Social Security Act passed Congress, and FDR signed it into law on August 14, 1935, the day before Will died.

Will repeatedly called for "relief for the farmer." In 1933, President Roosevelt signed the first "Farm Bill." Since then, farm bills have been passed by Congress every five years. Recent versions have allocated about 80 percent of the total budget to provide food for people experiencing poverty. Will would be pleased.

Will influenced humorists, comedians, and other entertainers with his authentic style. He had common sense and was the same person on stage as off. A handsome young actor, Joel McCrea, arrived in Hollywood. He made two movies with Will (Lightin' and Business and Pleasure). Will advised him to invest his money, "Invest half and live off the other half."

Joel McCrea bought a 1,000-acre ranch near Los Angeles in 1933, eventually expanding it to 2,300 acres. Most of that land is now part of the city of Thousand Oaks. Joel was glad he followed Will's advice. After Joel's death in 1990, the remaining 230 acres of the ranch, along with the house and other buildings, were donated to the Conejo Recreation and Park District for preservation.

Wyatt McCrea and Jennifer Rogers continue to keep the family friendship alive.

Will's newspaper columns influenced ordinary citizens and politicians. He shared his observations in plain language that ordinary people could understand and usually agree with. He used humor to make a point.

Jennifer's comment: In today's world, "Influencer" has a new meaning. On social media, it's all about who can get the most followers, so they can be paid to promote a particular product. The more followers, the more money. An influencer may not be a leader. However, Will Rogers was both, intending to be neither. His words brought comfort, influencing people to do the right thing. They gained respect for him and looked at him as a leader. It would be hard today to find one person who could influence the public, followed by good leadership. My good friend and mentor Jim Stovall has said, "If you want to be a leader, then surround yourself with leaders. Learn from their mistakes, ask them for advice, for they know what it takes to be a leader."

Randall's comment: We have an abundance of "Influencers" online today. But are they influencing for the future good, or mainly to sell an overpriced product? We have a few true "thought leaders" and many others who claim that title. It takes special skill, insight, and knowledge to visualize the future and persuade leaders (and followers) to act. You would not expect a cowboy with a tenth-grade education to qualify. As my friend, Scott McKain, who shares a birth date of November 4 with Will Rogers, told me, "Will was the definition of distinctive!!"

CHAPTER 2

LISTENER (AND ADMIT WHEN YOU ARE WRONG)

Will Rogers didn't always listen. But in 1903, in South Africa, Will listened and learned about show business from Texas Jack while performing with "Texas Jack's Wild West Show." "He gave me the idea for my original stage act with my pony. I used to study him by the hour, and from him I learned the great secret of show business: knowing when to get off."

He left South Africa not to return home, but to go to Australia and New Zealand to perform with The Wirth Brothers Circus. While there, performing as the "Cherokee Kid," the owner's wife made him a bright red velvet outfit. It was skin-tight and decorated with gold braids. Will liked the fancy clothing. When he finally returned home, he got to perform with "Zack Mulhall's Wild West Show" in St. Louis. He learned that Betty Blake, the young woman who would become his wife four years later, would attend the show with one of her sisters and a cousin.

Will proudly wore the red velvet get-up while doing rope tricks on his favorite horse. Oh my! Betty was horrified and embarrassed that the ordinary, common-sense cowboy she knew from Oologah would wear such a garish outfit. Will listened; he never wore the red velvet suit again.

In 1916, while performing on the Ziegfeld Follies vaudeville show, Will listened to Betty again (now his wife) and Florenz Ziegfeld when they suggested he talk during his act instead of doing rope tricks silently.

He listened to financier Bernard Baruch, who told him to avoid the Stock Market in 1928–29. A year before the stock market crashed in October 1929, Will warned the country, "You will try and show that we are prosperous because we HAVE MORE. I will show where we are NOT prosperous because we haven't PAID for it YET." (Life magazine, August 9, 1928)

Will Rogers listened to critics and admitted when he was wrong. After writing a column criticizing holding companies, including, "a holding company is like a fellow handing the other fellow the swag while they search you," he admitted he didn't know anything about holding companies. He even printed comments from a dozen letters criticizing him: "Now you will say, why did you pop off when you didn't know what you were talking about? Well, if you are going to stop that, why America would be speechless." (WA #640, March 31, 1935)

Jennifer's comment: One of the most asked questions I get about my great-grandfather is, "How did he raise his children?" By this, they are asking, was he the disciplinarian, or was Betty? Did he sit with his children and listen about their day, their school, their problems? I can only answer from what my grandfather, Jim Rogers, shared over the years. He always said, "When dad was home from being away making a movie or traveling, he was not Will Rogers; he was DAD and spent every moment with us kids." That leads me to believe that Will did listen to his children. My grandfather, Jim, and his siblings, Will, Jr. and Mary, were all raised humbly. My grandfather was by far the best listener I've ever known. I used to go to him with issues, concerns, and questions. He would sit for what felt like an eternity and never say a word until I was about ready to leave, and then for the next hour, he would give his two cents worth, which I always took. This was a trait passed down from his dad. However, Will wouldn't have sat for that long without giving his opinion.

Randall's comment: Listening is a skill that's not taught in school. However, being a good listener is a key to personal growth. Like Will's example with Texas Jack, you learn more when listening instead of talking. When Will listened to Betty, he learned to be his authentic self and not try to show off as an imposter. Even when acting in a movie, Will played himself. For most of us, being our authentic selves is important, except, in my case, when I'm pretending to be Will Rogers.

CHAPTER 3

PERSEVERANCE, PERSISTENCE, RECOVER FROM DISAPPOINTMENTS, CORRECT MISTAKES, AND MOVE ON

When Will was 22, he sold his cattle and went to The Argentine (Argentina). He was fascinated by what he had read and heard about the gauchos and wide-open range. His father, Clem Rogers, was against this wild journey, but he relented and paid Will $3,000 for his cattle to fund the trip.

To shorten the story, after a few weeks of exploring the cattle industry in the interior of the country, Will wrote a letter to his family admitting, "It's no place to make money unless you have $10,000 to invest." Will ran out of money, but instead of returning home, he got a job on a ship taking a load of cattle, mules, and other livestock to South Africa (you read about Texas Jack and the Wirth Brothers in the previous chapter).

While working for the Wirth Brothers Circus in Australia, Will had saved enough money to sail across the Pacific to California. Unfortunately, he got conned into a poker game and lost it all. He persevered and kept performing for eight more months. Finally, he had enough cash for a ticket on a steamship to San Francisco, "bottom class, instead of first class."

While doing the Ziegfeld Follies, he lived a while on Long Island along the coast. He enjoyed swimming at an inlet. One morning, he didn't notice that the tide had gone out. He dove into the shallow water, hit his head on a rock, and was unconscious. His right arm was paralyzed.

Incredibly, he practiced rope tricks with his left hand for hours and performed the same night. He never missed a show. His right arm recovered in a month. And now, Will Rogers could perform rope tricks with both hands! In "The Ropin' Fool," he tossed three lassos using both hands, catching different parts of a horse and the rider moving past him.

After being in several silent films starting in 1918, Will decided in 1921 that he knew enough about the business to produce and star in his own movies. He made three, including "The Ropin' Fool." He borrowed heavily to pay all production costs, including hiring other actors.

Unfortunately, he had not noticed that the movie theater chains preferred to show movies produced by their owners. They did not want any independent producers horning in on their business. An independent producer, Pathe, managed to get Will's films into a few theaters. But in two years, Will had only recouped about half of his expenses.

So, how did he persevere and recover? To help avoid bankruptcy, he turned to professional speaking, or, as Will called it, giving "lectures" on the speaking circuit. Will was well-known and was able to arrange an incredible lineup of speaking engagements. He gave 60 talks in 60 days, traveling from town to town by train and automobile. He was probably paid $1,000 for each speech. That unbelievable schedule got him out of a hole and made him a better professional speaker.

Also, at the end of 1922, he signed a contract with McNaught Syndicate to write one article a week. The first one was published in newspapers nationwide on December 24, 1922. "Weekly Articles" appeared mainly in Sunday papers on the op-ed page. These continued until his death on August 15, 1935, at Point Barrow, Alaska, totaling 665. The last four of these were written during his Alaska journey with Wiley Post and published in the weeks after his death.

Another column (No. 666), recovered from his typewriter after the airplane crashed into the shallow water, was not published until June 1941. One line in that Weekly Article is, "...we're headed for Point Barrow, the furthermost north of any piece of land on the North American Continent."

Have you ever been in an airplane crash, even a minor one? Will Rogers survived at least six "mishaps," including two on one trip. He did not survive the crash in Alaska.

Will Rogers had his first ride in an airplane in 1915. He supported aviation in its early, somewhat risky years. He recognized the value of speed, getting from one city to another. "If your time is worth anything, travel by air. If not, you might as well walk." (DT #389, October 20, 1927)

The U.S. had scheduled airmail routes before regular passenger plane routes. Will got permission from the Department of Commerce, headed by Secretary Herbert Hoover, to fly on the mail planes; he paid by the pound.

He was inducted into the National Aviation Hall of Fame in 1977 for his promotion of air travel. He is one of a few who were not pilots or involved directly in the industry.

Note: No U.S. President flew until FDR in 1943. Mrs. Roosevelt was the first First Lady to fly in July 1933. When she landed in Los Angeles, Will Rogers was there to greet her.

Will survived a near-death experience in San Francisco. He and a friend were in a hotel. It had gas lights in the room. Will had no experience with gas lights, only kerosene lanterns. So, he "blew out" the light instead of turning off the gas supply. In the hospital, the older doctors thought he was dead and gave up on him. Fortunately, young medical students were working with the doctors and did not give up. They got Will breathing again. It took a month for Will to fully recover.

Freddie, Will's youngest son, died of diphtheria in 1920, at 23 months of age. Will performed his show, as scheduled, later the same day. This commitment was a prime example of "the show must go on."

Jennifer's comment: My fifth-grade school teacher at Buena Vista Elementary in Tucumcari, New Mexico, was Ms. Webb. I remember her well, maybe because I was her favorite student. She always let me sit where I wanted, and let me pick up and pass out papers to the other students. I still have a note she gave me on the last day of school.

My mom often reminds me of her encouraging words for my future. She commented that I was a ray of sunshine that would lead me to great things in life. I'm not sure why I remember this, but I have always looked at the glass half full, not half empty.

My dearest friends will tell you I believe in being positive and forward momentum. This isn't always an easy choice, and for the first time in my adult life, I am leaning on others to help me continue moving forward. With the sudden loss of Will's Ranch in California and life-changing events in my personal life, I am trying to feed myself my own words. However, when we look at things in our lives, others always deal with greater devastation. Will had tremendous loss in his life. Betty writes in her book that Will never got over the loss of his mother, and only to lose a child must have been unbearable. As noted, he continued moving forward after so many setbacks. I have yet to read where he ever retreated in all the writings by and about

Will. The more I learn about my great-grandfather, the more I find how gifted he was.

Randall's comment: Will's friend Henry Ford said, "Failure is the opportunity to begin again more intelligently." Will did not give up after losing money in a poker game, as a movie producer, or being slightly injured when the airplane he was on flipped upside down when it landed. He persevered.

CHAPTER 4

NEW TECHNOLOGIES

Will Rogers was an "early adopter" of several technologies, including silent movies (including slow motion), radio, telegraph, talking movies, and airplane travel.

For "The Ropin' Fool," Will figured out how to speed up the movie camera to make his rope tricks believable. In the days of silent movies, the camera was cranked by hand. A camera operator would "over-crank" the camera to achieve slow motion, potentially cranking it at two or three times the normal speed. For "The Ropin' Fool," the camera operator cranked it at least five times the normal speed.

Will was featured in about 50 silent movies. But when the movies added sound in 1927, Will became an immediate star. He was in 21 "talkies" and was the highest-paid actor from 1933 until his death in 1935.

When Will was asked to write a daily article for newspapers in 1926, he sent them by telegraph. These short articles needed to arrive at the New York Times by 6:00 p.m. to get into morning papers across the country. These topical articles, often 50 to 100 words, became known as Daily Telegrams. By comparison, the Weekly Articles he had been writing since 1922 were much longer and were mailed to the syndicator. They usually appeared in Sunday newspapers about two weeks after he wrote them.

Of course, we're accustomed to receiving our "news" instantly today. Computers, the internet, and smartphones have replaced typewriters.

As described in the previous chapter, Will was an early supporter of air travel.

Top Army and Navy officials (and Congress in 1924) insisted that airplanes would have no role in future wars. Will wrote, "House of Representatives were arguing on whether we could raise the elevation of the guns on our battleships... if you are allowed to have a gun at all, you certainly ought to be allowed to point it any way that will get you the most good out of it. But most of them thought as our guns had always pointed toward the water instead of up in the air, why naturally, they should be kept pointing that way." (WA #78, June 8, 1924)

Will became friends with General Billy Mitchell, who was court-martialed in 1925 for insisting that airplanes might be important in winning a war.

"Aviation is not a fad; it's a necessity and will be our mode of travel long after all the people who are too valuable to fly have met their desired deaths by the roadsides on Sunday afternoons." (DT #809, February 28, 1929)

KDKA in Pittsburgh was the first radio station. Will appeared on KDKA two years later, in 1922. In 1927, the NBC radio network premiered nationwide with a big show with a half dozen stars. Will was the Master of Ceremonies. In 1930, E. R. Squibb & Sons signed Will to do 14 Sunday night shows for 15 minutes on a nationwide network.

From 1933 until June 1935, Gulf Oil sponsored 53 of the broadcasts. Will insisted on having a live audience to get reactions and laughs. He was totally unscripted. He would often invite famous audience members to the microphone and interview them. This was the beginning of "talk radio" and the format for late-night TV shows.

Will's most prominent radio broadcast was on October 18, 1931. He was part of the "President's Organization on Unemployment Relief" broadcast with President Hoover. He had several memorable quotes. "The only problem that confronts this country today is at least 7,000,000 men are out of work." After pointing out that we are blessed with "more wheat and more corn and more money in the bank," Will added, "we've got people starving. We'll hold the distinction of being the only nation in the history of the world that ever went to the poor house in an automobile."

Even though color photography existed, there are no color photos of Will. And Technicolor movies started four years after his death (Gone with the Wind, 1939).

Jennifer's comment: Ahh, Will and technology. What would Will think about technology today is another common question that I get and is hard to answer. I believe he would be great friends with Richard Branson and one of the first to travel to space. Always on the cutting edge of technology, Will was well ahead of his time. He saw the future of aviation and the role it would play in the next war.

While building his dream ranch in Pacific Palisades, California, Will used the latest technology. He had a state-of-the-art kitchen, historic oversized windows, and custom carvings of horseheads in beams supporting the beautiful patio. He built a barn for his horses that was unlike many in today's modern world until it burned on January 7, 2025. If it was new and exciting, Will had to have it or at least go see it. Will believed that technology and its efficiencies were necessary to move forward in an uncharted world.

Randall's comment: Many of us remember when we saw or bought our first color TV, handheld calculator, desktop computer, microwave oven, cellular phone, digital camera, VHS tape, or smartphone. Today, we have Artificial Intelligence (AI) and other new technologies that come out every few weeks, and if we don't grab on and embrace them, we can be left behind. In many cases, waiting a few months for the bugs to be worked out and the price to drop is best. And the perfect time to buy is when you have a young granddaughter to explain and show you how it works!

CHAPTER 5

READING AND ASSOCIATING WITH SMARTER PEOPLE

"All I know is what I read in the newspaper." Will Rogers often began his presentations and newspaper articles with this quote. He had always depended on newspapers to keep him informed. Will depended greatly on newspapers for fresh material when he began headlining the Ziegfeld Frolic, a midnight show that followed the Ziegfeld Follies. Will was on both, and many in the audience for the midnight show had also been in the audience for the Follies. So, he had to come up with new material.

Betty suggested that he should comment on what he had read in the newspaper. He arranged for the morning editions of New York City newspapers to be delivered at 11:00 p.m. When he went on the Frolic at midnight, he had new material to present with a humorous twist. Literally, he informed his audience ahead of the news they would read hours later.

"A breakfast without a newspaper is a Horse without a Saddle. You are riding bareback if you got no news for breakfast." (WA #480, March 6, 1932)

"Of late, all I am asked is: 'Who writes your stuff, and where do you get it?' And the surprising answer is: The newspapers write it! All I do is to get all the papers I can carry and then read all that is going on and try to figure out the main things that the audience has read, and talk on that. I have found out two things.

One is that the more up-to-date a subject is the more credit you are given for talking on it, even if you haven't anything funny. But if it is an old subject, your gags must be funny to get over.... The first thing is the remark you make must be founded on facts. You can exaggerate and make it ridiculous, but it must have the plain facts in it. Then you will hear the audience say: 'Well, that's pretty near right.'" (How To Be Funny, July 1917)

Will praised the editors of small-town and weekly newspapers, "They are not conceited enough to think they 'mold public opinion.' They go along serving their community with the most indispensable article that it has. And yet their real power is greater than all your metropolitan dailies combined. Any person that don't read at least one well-written country newspaper is not truly informed." (DT #1865, July 27, 1932)

"A man (person) only learns by two things, one is reading, and the other is association with smarter people. I do hope I last long enough to reach your town. If it's got a railroad and a Town Hall we will be there sooner or later. I am going out among the people whom New Yorkers call Rubes. But these people I am going out among are the people that look at New Yorkers and laugh." (WA # 147, October 4, 1925)

The most successful leaders hire people smarter than they are. Will associated with smarter people, better informed people in all walks of life, including "Rubes."

Among his friends were Henry Ford, Amon Carter, Florenz Ziegfeld, Charlie Chaplin, John Ford, Herbert Hoover, Franklin D. Roosevelt, the Prince of Wales (Edward), Charles Lindbergh, Amelia Earhart, Annie Oakley, and several Congressmen, Senators, Governors and First Ladies.

Will was inspired by interactions with a wide assortment of leaders in business, state and federal government, foreign governments, journalism, Hollywood, and religious organizations. He was constantly learning from them and often shared that "new" knowledge on the stage and with his readers and radio listeners, often wrapped in humor.

We could fill a book with Will's conversations with, and observations about, a hundred of these leaders. Here are three examples:

On President Herbert Hoover: "I always did want to see him elected. I wanted to see how far a competent man could go in politics. It has never been tried before." (Radio, April 20, 1930)

On Henry Ford, who invented assembly line production for cars: "If there had never been a Ford car, there never would have been a cheap car.... Ford's success is due to the fact he uses common sense in his business instead of a board of directors. He shames a lot of the other concerns in paying high wages. He believes in giving a man a job." (Radio, June 1, 1930)

At the start of President Franklin Roosevelt's first term in office: "We have no precedent in the accomplishments which this man has performed in the last seven weeks. That bird has done more in seven weeks than we've done for ourselves in seven years." (Radio, April 30, 1933)

Jennifer's comment: It is no secret that Will was an avid reader. So was my grandfather, Jim, and my father, Kem. They always had a book in their hands. But Will read to get material for his audience and newspaper columns. One of my favorite quotes is, "A man only learns by two things, one is reading, and the other is association with smarter people." Sadly, the reading trait did not pass down to me. In my office, I have over 100 books that, over the years, have been given to me by amazing authors. I intend to read them, but I am much happier having a conversation with someone, learning from them, and picking their brains rather than nestled in a book. I have learned that many of my biggest lessons have come from associating with smarter people.

Randall's comment: Unfortunately, newspapers (print versions) are losing business to digital sources, including television. Will Rogers read different newspapers, so he had access to different views. Today, we need to get our news from various angles, not one. I'm glad that Will's hometown newspaper, The Claremore Progress, is still thriving. And I read the weekly newspaper I grew up with, the Weston Democrat. Fortunately, we still have "smarter people" with whom to associate. Sometimes, it's challenging to separate those who are merely smart from the ones with common horse sense.

CHAPTER 6

HAVE FUN, BE INTERESTING, LIKEABLE, AND HUMBLE. STAY HEALTHY

Will Rogers was a brilliant person with a high IQ. He could have a serious conversation on an important topic if the situation required it, and he could write a column or a business letter in perfect English.

But mostly, he was authentic to his roots, from growing up as a quarter-blood Cherokee on a ranch in Indian Territory. “I am an old country boy in a big town trying to get along. I have been eating pretty regular, and the reason I have been is because I have stayed an old country boy.” (WA #90, August 31, 1924)

Once, during the Great Depression, he was criticized for bad grammar in his syndicated newspaper columns. He responded, “I know a lot of people who never say ain’t that ain’t eatin’.”

Will’s best-known quote is, “I never met a man I didn’t like.” He was referring mainly to prominent leaders he met across the nation and around the world. But he was referring to almost everyone, including women. The key word in that quote is “met.” When you first meet someone, don’t be turned off by their physical appearance or perhaps a disparaging remark (gossip) you heard from someone else. Give everyone a fair first chance to be a friend. Now, after you get acquainted, you don’t have to like them if they turn out to be a scoundrel, horse thief, or a dictator.

Will joked about prominent men, including Presidents. If one took offense, it hurt Will's feelings, and he would immediately apologize. In a skit on the Ziegfeld Follies, Will had a line that poked fun at President Harding for playing a lot of golf. Answering a (pretend) phone call from the President, Will said, "Hello… Mr. Harding?… You say you lost by two holes? Well, you can't win every day."

One day, a secretary from the White House stopped by and asked Will to stop the joke because people were repeating it all over Washington. This hurt Will. He never thought a President would be upset at his jokes. He never used that line again. A few days later, he told the audience at the Follies, "I have cracked jokes on both Republicans and Democrats. I hope I have not given offense. In fact, I don't believe any big man will take offense."

Years later, he wrote, "I have often said in answer to inquiries as to how I got away with kidding some of our public men, that it was because I liked all of them personally, and that if there was no malice in your heart there could be none in your 'Gags,' and I have always said I never met a man I didn't like." (WA #372, February 9, 1930)

"There ain't nothing to life but satisfaction." (July 5, 1931)

"To be successful you've got to know what you're doing, believe in what you're doing and love what you're doing." A young lawyer, Cavett Robert, who founded the National Speakers Association in 1973, wrote down this quote by Will when he spoke at a convention of the American Bar Association in 1935.

When Will was home, he was totally with the family. He left his work "at the office." He played with the kids and spent a lot of time riding his horses, roping calves, and playing polo. He would often say to Betty, "Let's go for a drive." She reflected that those drives, heading nowhere in particular, were among her most enjoyable moments. It's important to take time for yourself and your family.

Will nearly always included humor in his comments. He could criticize an official for a policy and then end with a touch of humor that made the "victim" smile or laugh. Or, the reverse: "Yes, Will was funny, but he was telling us something important."

During the Ziegfeld Follies, which featured more than a dozen beautiful young women, Will said, "In 20 years, they'll look 5 years older."

Staying healthy was important to Will. He did 100 Texas Skips most mornings. Doing 100 of those rope tricks would equal the endurance of most pro athletes. Will had at least 88 different rope tricks. These required physical and mental skills. A couple of them, included in the silent film "The Ropin' Fool," have never been duplicated.

Will spent his free time wisely. In the 1930s, he was contracted to make three movies a year. He wanted them to be done early in the year so he had time for travel.

Good health is important to live a long life. Of course, many men and women who die unexpectedly have great achievements. Many, perhaps most, who were great contributors to society have lived to be quite old. You will recognize these prominent men and women who had a connection to Will: John D. Rockefeller, Mark Twain, Henry Ford, Thomas Edison, Eleanor Roosevelt, and Albert Einstein.

Will Rogers was in excellent health. His only significant health problem occurred in 1927:

"It hadn't shown up in years, until one spring, on my tour of national annoyances, I hit a town called Bluefield, West Virginia. Now ordinarily when a pain hits you in the stomach in Bluefield, West Virginia, you would take it for gunshot wounds. But the old town has quieted down now and the sharpshooters have all joined the Kiwanis and Rotary Clubs. So, I knew it wasn't wounds. Then the pain struck me before the nightly lecture and I knew no one would shoot me before the lecture, unless by chance he had heard it over in another town." (Ether and Me, 1929)

Days later, back home in California, Betty got him into a hospital. He had gallstones removed in surgery which was more serious than he realized. He wrote a 32-page book about the experience, "Ether and Me or Just Relax." Of course, he praised the doctors who operated on him. But this quote from the book is popular with animal doctors, "Personally, I have always felt that the best doctor in the world is the Veterinarian. He can't ask his patients what is the matter—he's got to just know."

If not for the fatal airplane crash when he was 55, Will could easily have lived 20 more years. His dad, Clem Rogers, died at 74. His oldest sister, Sallie Rogers McSpadden, lived to be 80.

Jennifer's comment: Will lived each day to the fullest. I remember doing an interview when I was asked what I thought about Will dying at such a young age but having accomplished so much in his 55 short years. As I thought about my answer, I became extremely emotional, realizing I was 55 years old as I sat there! I began to reflect on my accomplishments and realized I better get a move on. Because of all the people Will met and the places he traveled, his bag of interesting conversations never ran short. He never met a stranger. At the end of the day, he was that same boy from a ranch in Indian Territory, and he never let himself forget it. May we all be so humble.

Randall's comment: Will Rogers was a master at adding or responding with humor. Occasionally, I interject a smile or laughter to help lighten the mood. With almost any interaction with a person or group, give them something to smile or laugh about. Even a simple, friendly smile as you pass someone in the hall or on a sidewalk often gets a smile in return. As Will said, "Get a few laughs, do the best you can."

CHAPTER 7

LEADERS ARE COMFORTERS

Will Rogers • was compassionate and generous with his time and money. He comforted friends, people he worked with in the movie business, and anyone across the country and worldwide who was suffering hardship. Here are five examples as described by Will in his syndicated newspaper columns: floods in the Mississippi Valley, drought in Texas and Oklahoma, earthquake in Nicaragua, theater fire in Ireland, and a sick boy in New Mexico.

"I don't believe our people that have never been around a flood area realize the tremendous need of these sufferers down on the Mississippi. It's by far the worst thing that has happened in this country in years... Now, we have a chance to help the poorest people in America, and that is the renter farmer. Mr. Ziegfeld has generously given me his wonderful new theatre in New York City, and I am going to put on my little one-man [show] for this great cause next Sunday night... They will get every cent that comes in, even if there is nobody there but my wife—who will have to pay to get in." (DT #236, April 25, 1927)

"These people in the drought-stricken country ain't waiting for the government to relieve 'em. Their well-to-do are helping the less fortunate themselves. At a matinee today in Wichita Falls, we [raised] $9,100. At Fort Worth tonight, $18,000. At Abilene, got

$6,500, and every cent of that is net. People in America have got the money and will give if they know the need is there." (DT #1411, January 30, 1931)

Will was in Nicaragua eight days after a major earthquake left thousands homeless and without food. He donated $5,000 himself.

"Well, here we are at Managua, Nicaragua… The Red Cross combined with the relief organization here has done great work as usual and still is. They are feeding about 8,000… If you saw, as I did this morning, 2,500 mothers with babies in their arms go by and get their ration of milk you would say there was some poor devil that needed it worse than you do." (WA #1469, April 8, 1931)

While performing in London, England, he heard about a movie theater fire in Dromcolliher, Ireland that killed 46 people. He sent a telegram to the President of Ireland (yes, a leader with a title), and in two days, they organized a full show and raised $4000.

"I want to tell you I have been mixed up in all kinds of shows but this one last night was the greatest one I ever was in. You talk about an audience! They were packed in!... They were without a doubt the most appreciative audience I ever saw in my life." (WA #198, September 26, 1926)

On a smaller scale, Will made an impact on a family when he stayed at a small motel along Route 66 in Santa Rosa, New Mexico. The owner's son was sick, so he asked Will if he would go to the boy's bedside and say a few comforting words. Will gladly agreed and talked with the son for quite a while. The next morning, the boy was feeling good and seemingly recovered. The owner was so thrilled he asked Will if he would let him change the name to "Will Rogers Motel."

Jennifer's comment: Good leaders inspire excellence and reduce friction. Will did both.

People felt at ease with him. As mentioned above, there are multiple examples and stories of Will bringing comfort to countless people and countries. I have always wondered what pressure that put on the man. If I could have five minutes with him, I would ask, "When did you find time to take care of yourself?"

As the representative of the Rogers family, I have opportunities to travel and meet some amazing people. I get invited to unique and special events and have made friendships that will last a lifetime. But it wasn't until the devastating fire that took Will's beautiful ranch house at Will Rogers State Historic Park on January 7, 2025, that my role was most challenged. Having moved to Claremore, Oklahoma, and living a block away from the Will Rogers Memorial Museum, where Will and his family, including my father, are interred, I sat in disbelief as I was given detail by detail of the fire's destruction as it moved from the historic stables sweeping down over the beautiful lawn eventually taking the historic house and most of its contents.

As I wept and spoke to Will and Betty, apologizing for not being able to save the historic home, I found myself in Will's shoes. Immediately, the phone calls began, followed by hundreds of emails and press interviews that are still ongoing. The following morning, I arrived at the Memorial Museum, seeking comfort from staff and volunteers. Most of them had visited the ranch at one time or another. I was holding back the tears as they all met me at the door. What I quickly learned was that they needed ME!

I had never before felt the presence of my great-grandfather until that moment. I knew then I needed to put aside my emotions and comfort them and theirs. I have no idea how Will did this on a daily basis. That moment taught me that he was even more special than I ever imagined. He had an inner strength that is extremely rare and a gift that many took for granted. As my journey continues, keeping his legacy alive, I do so now with much more grace and respect. How proud I am to have finally met my great-grandfather!

WILL ROGERS MEMORIAL MUSEUM, CLAREMORE, OK AND WILL ROGERS STATE HISTORIC PARK, PACIFIC PALISADES, CA

Will Rogers Memorial Museum is located in Claremore, Oklahoma. The museum is the final resting place of Will and Betty, along with 3 of their children and a grandchild. The Memorial Museum displays an exclusive collection of Will's life including everything from artwork to his saddle collection. The museum hosts visitors from around the world.

Will Rogers State Historic Park, located in Pacific Palisades, has played host to the Will Rogers Polo Club and an extensive horseback riding program. It is the hope that in the near future these activities can once again entertain visitors and be the amazing escape to the busy life of the Los Angeles area.

To learn more and stay updated, please visit www.WillRogers.com

ABOUT THE AUTHORS

Jennifer Rogers is a proud great-granddaughter of Will Rogers. She began her involvement in the Rogers family business in 1991 after attending the nine-time Tony Award winner "The Will Rogers Follies" on Broadway. Jennifer now serves as the family spokesperson and travels throughout the year promoting the legacy of Will Rogers.

In 2006, Jennifer co-founded the Will Rogers Ranch Foundation, supporting the

186-acre Will Rogers State Historic Park in Pacific Palisades, California. Sadly, on January 7, 2025, the historic ranch house and stables were lost in the tragic Palisades fire that burned for three weeks and destroyed 6800 structures.

For 21 years, Jennifer owned and operated an almond company which produced and retailed flavored almonds. The label: "My Husband's Nuts." In 2024, she closed the business and began to focus all of her attention promoting the legacy of her great-grandfather.

Jennifer is now residing in Claremore, Oklahoma, where she is active in the Will Rogers Memorial Museum. She still spends time devoted to continuing the legacy of Will at the California ranch. She is also active in preserving historic U.S. Route 66, aka The Will Rogers Highway, which is celebrating its 100th anniversary in 2026.

A highlight of Jennifer's family involvement was having the opportunity to represent

Will Rogers by riding horseback in the Rose Parade in Pasadena with a group called "Sons and Daughters of the Reel West."

In addition to the Will Rogers Ranch Foundation, Jennifer is an active board member serving on the Will Rogers Memorial Museum Foundation, Will Rogers Motion Picture Pioneers Foundation and The National Cowboy and Western Heritage Museum.

She is a proud mother to Meeghan and son-in-law Dominic Sill, and Mason and daughter-in-law Mekayla Etcheverry. She has three grandchildren and promises to help them grow up to honor and cherish their great-great-great-grandfather, Will Rogers.

Randall Reeder has been speaking as "Will Rogers" since 1996 when he was "discovered" by an Oklahoma professional speaker, Dale Minnick. He told Randall that "God put you together to remind us of the most admired man in the U.S. in the 20th Century." Although Randall does not claim to live up to that high calling, he presents programs to businesses and organizations across the country as "Will Rogers." And he writes a "Weekly Comments" in Will Rogers style. (Available at: WillRogersToday.com.)

In 2013, Randall published a book of Will Rogers' quotes and stories about agriculture, called "I Never Met a Farmer I Didn't Like."

Randall grew up on a small livestock farm in West Virginia. He graduated from West Virginia University in the College of Engineering. From 1979 to 2011, he was on the faculty at Ohio State University as an Extension Agricultural Engineer.

At Ohio State, Randall worked with farm machinery, conservation tillage systems, energy, and 4-H youth programs. He is a member of the National Speakers Association, National Society of Professional Engineers, and American Farm Bureau Federation. He currently serves as Executive Director of the Ohio No-till Council and Vice-President of the National No-till Farmer Foundation.

LIFE-CHANGING CLASSICS SERIES

3 Therapies of Life (The), by Charlie "Tremendous" Jones. Renowned speaker and bestselling author Charlie "Tremendous" Jones shares a wealth of knowledge from decades of experience in business and life.

7 Golden Rules of Milton Hershey (The), by Greg Rothman. This book is a collection of the wisdom that set this great American industrialist apart from most of his robber-baron contemporaries.

7 Leadership Virtues of Joan of Arc (The), by Peter Darcy. A powerful catalog of the traits that made a mark on history. This small book tells the tale of her leadership virtues as a mystic and a warrior who obeyed the command of God to perform extraordinary deeds.

Acres of Diamonds, by Russell H. Conwell. This gem of a book will help you to discover why Temple University founder Russell Conwell was referred to as the penniless millionaire and how he helped millions of others tap into their potential through his famous *Acres of Diamonds* speech.

Advantages of Poverty, by Andrew Carnegie; Foreword by Dale Carnegie. Discover the attitude of selfless giving that motivated this innovative businessman to help various communities, charities and organizations achieve greater success.

As a Man Thinketh, by James Allen. Og Mandino counted *As a Man Thinketh* among the top ten success books of all time. All that we achieve and all that we fail to achieve is the direct result of our own thoughts.

Books Are Tremendous, edited by Charlie "Tremendous" Jones. This book documents the amazing impact that the reading of good books has had on great men and women throughout history. As you read the inspirational words by some of these influential individuals who have been transformed by the power of the written word, they will undoubtedly inspire you to develop a far greater appreciation for reading.

"Bradford, You're Fired!" by William W. Woodbridge. This is a timeless classic containing a provocative story of "The Superself" that exists in every person who is willing to take an honest assessment of his or her life in order to make change for the better realizing every one of us is in business for ourselves.

Breakthrough Speaking, by Mark Sanborn. Anyone with the courage to speak publicly can deliver a speech, but breakthrough speakers inspire listeners to take action. If you have a message to deliver – one that you sincerely believe in – and your philosophy moves you to want to inspire and change people, the best way to reach them is by mastering *Breakthrough Speaking*!

Character Building, by Booker T. Washington. This practical book by the former slave and founder of Tuskegee Institute shares keys to character building taken from the notes he compiled related to his *Sunday Evening* Talks to students and teachers during the early days of the Institute.

Discipleship, by John M. Segal. John shares his understanding of the difference between discipleship and salvation, and what that means for people in today's culture. His plain language approach openly states his early perspective of hypocrisy in the church, and how his attempt for spiritual growth brought him to the truth in scripture.

Frank Perdue Way: Simple Steps, Super Success, by Mitzi Perdue. You know Frank Perdue as the CEO spokesperson in his innovative television ads claiming, "It takes a tough man to make a tender chicken." He was a captain of industry, a philanthropist, a loving family man, and a true American success story if there ever was one. How did he do it? And much more importantly, what did he do that you can do, too?

From Belfast to Narnia: The Life and Faith of C.S. Lewis, by The C.S. Lewis Institute. In this brief introduction to his life and works you will uncover what inspired C.S. Lewis, what drove him and what experiences shaped the life of this extraordinary writer, theologian and friend of God.

Greatest Thing in the World (The), by Henry Drummond. This classic book illuminates the importance of 1 Corinthians 13. Widely read and quoted for decades, it has sold millions of copies and continues to influence people to follow God's two great commandments: to love God and to love each other.

Key to Excellence (The), by Charlie "Tremendous" Jones. Filled with classic wisdom and humor, this easy-to-read book reflects Charlie's keys to excellence in Leadership, ministry, home, and work.

Kingship of Self-Control (The), by William George Jordan. This a book that will lead you expertly along the road of personal triumph by pointing the way to ultimate growth and happiness through self-discipline.

Lincoln Ideals (The), edited by Charlie "Tremendous" Jones. This remarkable, pocket-sized collection of excerpts and quotes in Lincoln's own words provides an inspiring insight into the mind of our greatest president.

Love of God (The), by Charlie "Tremendous" Jones. Renowned speaker and bestselling author Charlie "Tremendous" Jones shares how he went from believing there was no such thing as love to finding its actual source. Charlie entered the world as a broken child who later became a successful husband, father, and life insurance salesman.

Luther on Leadership, by Stephen J. Nichols. This volume in the Life-Changing Classics series outlines five leadership tenets of Martin Luther, the man whose theological trajectory allowed millions to find a personal relationship with God.

Maxims of Life & Business With Selected Prayers. This is a dynamic book that encapsulates the life and wisdom of John Wanamaker. The wisdom of the millionaire "Merchant Prince" who was the originator of the department store concept will undoubtedly inspire you to live your life to the fullest and for the benefit of others.

Message to Garcia (A), by Elbert Hubbard. A Message to Garcia, one of the keystones of American self-improvement literature, has carried its simple message of hard work, integrity and dependability to readers around the world for over 100 years.

My Conversion, by Charles Spurgeon. A classic account of his coming to understand the plan of salvation, now available in our popular *Laws of Leadership* series!

Mystery of Self-Motivation (The), by Charlie "Tremendous" Jones. There are no barriers you can't overcome if you are learning to be motivated.

New Common Denominator of Success (The), by Albert E.N. Gray. The common denominator of success, the secret of success of every person who has ever been successful lies in the fact that he or she formed the habit of doing things that failures don't like to do.

Price of Leadership (The), by Charlie "Tremendous" Jones; foreword by Tracey Jones. Experience nonstop laughter as you experience this great humanitarian's ideas about life's most challenging situations in business and at home.

Reason Why (The), by R.A. Laidlaw; Introduction by Marjorie Blanchard. R. A. Laidlaw, a highly successful New Zealand businessman, shares his faith with his employees. *The Reason Why* is just as essential and compelling today as it was over ninety years ago.

Ronald Wilson Reagan: The Great Communicator, by Greg Rothman. A brief yet compelling biography by Greg Rothman that unveils the human being behind the man who magnificently played the role of leader of the free world.

Science of Getting Rich: Abridged Edition (The), by Wallace D. Wattles. Men get rich by doing things in a Certain Way; and in order to do so, men must become able to think in a certain way. A man's way of doing things is the direct result of the way he thinks about things.

Self-Improvement Through Public Speaking, by Orison Swett Marden. Research has confirmed again and again that public speaking is essential to success. This practical guide will help you to understand the significance of gaining the verbal advantage needed for your career, personal, and social life.

Succeeding With What You Have, by Charles Schwab; Foreword by Andrew Carnegie. Schwab had a deep appreciation for the common, dedicated working man and he gave the power to succeed to any employee who was willing to pay the price.

That Something, by William W. Woodbridge. *That Something* is real power as truly as the electric current . . . it is the power of the inner being, the fuel of the soul machine . . . it is the one thing necessary.

Three Decisions (The), by Charlie "Tremendous" Jones. This book shows us that, when we clear away the clutter that fills our daily existence, we'll find that there are only three decisions that determine the course of each of our lives. What are they? Read *The Three Decisions* and find out!

Walt Disney: Dreams Really Do Come True!, by Jason Liller. Learn some of Walt's secrets of success in these pages, apply them to your life right now, and build a wondrous future for yourself, your company, and your family!

Way to Wealth (The), by Benjamin Franklin. Discover the timeless wisdom of Benjamin Franklin in "The Way to Wealth," a powerful essay on personal finance and success. Originally published as a preface to *Poor Richard's Almanack* in 1758, this enduring work offers practical guidance on saving, investing wisely, and achieving financial independence.

Wit and Wisdom of General George S. Patton (The), compiled by Charlie "T." Jones. The wit and wisdom of one of our greatest military leaders in a compact, highly readable edition!